Echoes
From the Soul

Annie Baker

Dedicated to...
My Dad, who encouraged me to search,
and my son, Connor, who keeps me searching.

∾

www.anniebaker.com.au

Poems by: Annie Baker

Pictures by: Annie Baker and Unsplash

Special Thanks to: iwibooks.com

ISBN: 978-0-6450359-0-2

Contents

UNDER THE SHADOW OF THE YEW

Under the shadow of the Yew lies my father's ashes
 Resting beneath long, green lashes.
Over the Gresford churchyard the bells did toll,
 Welcoming another displaced, Welsh soul.

Death's shadow did float and roam
 Determined to return families home.
No earthly presence could stay time's hand
 Returning my father to his land.

For us left behind
  We must accept everyone has their time.
And, the person who occupied our very centre
  Has shifted his place to where we cannot enter.

To mourn his time of rest
  would mean to forsake the quest.
Trust there is a grand design
  Pain and loss has reason and rhyme.

Life to death, a letting go within.
  Know the light will never dim.
A flicker of the flame; a changing of roles,
  Mortal love must yield to the vacating soul.

All creation's creatures with every breath
  Step closer and closer to their death.
Make life then a joyful game,
  Moment to moment, not fear engrained.

The tree will continue to grow and spread,
  Memories transmitted and said.
So even after the deepest pain,
  Your heart can welcome life again.

FAIRY GLEN

Sitting quietly my mind back treads
Across a threshold of silken thread.
Passing through an eternal gate
Onto a path of altered state.
Via rocky slope my feet passed through,
Down softly spoken avenues.

To watery choirs raised in song
Through rocky corridors, coursing strong.
Into the silence, the gorge did descend;
Invisible forces that once did rend.

Far below on emerald moss,
Through cromlech portal, sprites did cross.
To tend and spritz with dragon's breath
Boulders large in pitch and breadth.

Mabon's oldest and wisest, spawned
Through Conwy's waters, leapt into dawn.
From fluent flow to falling foam,
They quested in search of home.

Gwrageth Annwn and Ellyllon
Enchant eddies and tourbillion,
Gossamer mists and cursive streams.
Under Fairy Glen glamour, I floated and dreamed.
In those waters, I dipped my feet;
Absorbed its life, my journey complete.

(Note: Welsh words pronounced Gra-geth Arn-oo & Eth-lth-lon representing the
water & valley/grove fairies)

6

AFTER THE RAIN

After the rain has gone,
I listen to the cool evening song.
The weavers of silken threads
Admire dew laden cobwebs;
Hammocks sagging between trees
And many craggy crannies.

Rainbow light
Filters through wooden catchments.
Their glistening green gaze
Sore from crafting a tapestry,
Angles for moistening tears
In the dawn receding night.

A cloak to cover a delicate work,
Till dedicated hands
For light will search
Continue to weave in misty lands
While time-weighed nodding heads
Slump into mossy beds.

In peace and silence,
Dream
Of the cleansing that has been borne.
Worlds converging in many streams,
Carrying life into the dawn
And all this sprouting from a storm.

ID

When winter touches my heart,

Summer must fill my soul.

Summon a strength everyone knows

In different ways, on different days.

On challenging paths.

VOICES

Strange voices on the wind
  That stir up the sky.
Pounding seas excited
  By passing birds' wailing cries.
With wings to span scaling oceans.

Velvet, grey cloaks of forgotten titans,
  threaten Archean stone blocks;
Sculpted by icy fingers that plummet
  From unwatched clocks.
Weapons to pierce the spirits of mortals.

Incantations sighed through unfolding hands
  Caress the bodies ebbing on distant shores.
Eyes hypnotically sway
  To breath that smells of change,
And fingers that carry the crispness of a transient rain.

It possesses a longing that invades the heart;
  Filled with the expressions of a million
Soft faces.
  Touched by the impressions
Of untold places.

Chimes growing for eons in time.
Voices of wisdom woven on the wind
And spoken by the seas.
Accomplices igniting the spark
That still lingers in you and me.

Of Gaia's life emerging.

The end of life;

The end of time.

WINDS

Moving life

Through branches of time…

Unceasing.

Carrying you forward,

Pushing you back.

Sculpting, ravaging,

Caressing.

A lullaby.

❧

A TOUCH OF AUTUMN

Glistening mornings tanged by frozen breezes
Transport dew to newly warmed green spears.
Sun-drenched mornings with the whisper of winter coming
On its lips.

Stirring oceans become restless and cold.
Touch young and old.
Carrying the inner secrets of summers gone.
A future winter's tale.

Bladed fingers of light cut an outline of gold
Through brown limbs tattooed by past seasons.
Reveal patches of summer's lingering
As cities prepare to combat autumn's warnings.

Soft velvet of moody condition
Fills with the sorrow of bidding farewell
To a friend of warm disposition.
Without refraining tears F
                        A
                          L
                        L

But dry your eyes my friend.
Autumn spreads its brown hue and golden tinsel
Over rolling, sequined bodies and
Flowing blue-grey calms,

C
  A
    R
      R
        Y
          I
            N
              G

Remainders
Of summer charms.

Watched by wishful green eyes
Unknowingly becoming
Mellow,
Yellow.
Dropping
To slide down living glass.
Coming to rest on tinted grass
Underneath, the browning roots of Autumn.

GOING HOME

Outstretched hands and smiling faces,
Aching hearts and warm embraces.
Comfort minds
Reflecting back home.
Remember happier times.
Feel they are never alone.

No stone left unturned.
Not a heart left unchanged.
Lessons pouring.
Spirits soaring.

WOULD IT NOT BE

A captured moment.
A fleeting glimpse.
Thoughts that wander.
Words eclipsed.

Could there not be
More silent thoughts?
Less voices caught.
Less perceptions wavering,
In pandemonium reigning.
Inspiration vibrating
Like a pendulum
Poised, and wrought.

Inner eyes that see,
Insight flows free.
Silence before the word.
Not too absurd.

Could it not?

YAN DONG SHAN

(Big Bird Gliding Mountain)

Toward a majesty that has no rival.
Where a spirit has no worry of survival.
Thru' bustling culture,
  A rickety bus rushes and roars
To pinnacles that plunge and soar.
A goddess' merciful finger rising,
  Against amber skies, beckons our arriving.
Beyond her cavernous core
  World woes settle, like shoes outside a door.

A threshold crossed and the faithful chanting.
Nature's temple and deity enchanting.
Notes off resonant stone
  Offer prayers to people at home.
Voices swirling thru' mountain mist
Blessings whispered,
  Into indigo light.
Candles lit,
  For footsteps, descending in the night.

Cradled within the Shan's breast.
And old monk who has laid the world to rest,
Face shaded under the Hood.
  Hand extended, on the threshold we stood.
Farewelled from another dimension.
Untouched by man's intervention.
  Moulded by the Tao's intention.
A gracious gift,
  And divine intervention.

SONATA

Sonorous rhythms.
Oscillating altercations.
Rushing resonances.
Twirling cadences.
Vocal cords leaping.
Voices of light-filled sound.
A choir of expectant children.
A nervous mother whittling.
An antediluvian father
Critical, dissatisfied,
Hopeful, proud.
A sublime orchestra.
Of skilled musicians,
Notes ebb and flow
In perfect harmony.

The overture fades.
So now,
Listen to the chorus.

❧

YEAR ONE

In the thicket by a brook,

sits a child of mirth and shining.

Year one,

Page one,

Turning.

Life, his story emerging.

BRETHREN

If there was not a tree

For all the world to see.

If there was not a rest

For a single bird to nest.

If grains of sand

Could not hold a strong, reassuring hand.

If a gaze upturned to the blue expanse

Could not see rich green eyes twinkle and dance.

Poor people indeed we would be.

To be without our brethren, trees.

HELIOS

A tropical haze
  Drifts through winter days.
Remember summers gone,
  When eyes heavy from the day
  Rested with thoughts lifted away.

Winged winds glided over burnished hills
  Cold from the night; eager for the light.
Chill seas sighed with welcomed warmth,
  Crests embalmed by the encroaching dawn,
  Spilt life like wine onto withering sands.

But the time is late
  Exhausted by the pace.
People abandon the land
  Salt and anguish etched into each face,
  And callousness scaring every hand.

Weather is quick to pass, but tides impossible to turn,
  And minds resistant to surrender.
Wandering winds rustle trees,
  Changing colours and schemes.
  People ever longing for the elusive green.

Welcomed fires will soon rekindle within
　From the seeping warmth of an ancient hearth.
Gaia, in homage, will rotate it's mantle.
　Dry life's tears from chilly depths,
　Thaw cold bodies to golden silhouettes.

From grey, grizzly swells
　To sparkling mirrors.
Deflect and quell
　The last wintry spells
　And troubles of a million winters.

PASSING TO NIGHT

Ocean in the sky
Echo with birds' fleeting cries
Seen through the twilight of dusk,
And clouds scented with the colour of musk.

Waves of misty foam wash
Shores sprinkled with mimosa.
Rows of spectral light
Splay out, a last attempt to repel the night.

Purple pillows coerce sea blue to slate grey,
Drawing river's heads away
Into a dark, cloudless expanse
Illumined by stellar radiance.

WHITE HORSES

White horses ride high

Through a limitless sky.

Down to mellowing hot sands,

Holding the ages of man.

Walking hand in hand,

You begin to understand

Why white horses are free

To line the boundaries of the sea.

❧

ODE TO MERRICKA

China moon
And a birthday soon.
The balance of a scale
For a Libran male.

Happy times
And funny lines.
A wandering minstrel
of air and crystal
Will celebrate with mirth,
his 31st birth.

With good friends and wine
Lots of happiness will find.
Each to take their places
To fill his empty spaces.

MEANDERINGS

Gusts transport my fears.
Clouds express my tears.
We look without seeing,
Touch without feeling
And kill without killing.

Someone prized,
elevated to the gallery wall.
Only one person asks why,
They rose while others did fall.
Why they basked within the halo
and others waned in shadow.

Those questions rarely asked,
Answers seldom heard.
Stand on a ledge of rock, stranded.
Only a forward path
Unchangeable, is earned.

The powerless climb an undetermined road
Seeking release from their heavy load.
Gold-embedded palms
Have no one to trust.
They walk the path alone
Until their bones turn to dust.
Their souls known no charms.
Hearts nourished by paper freshly grown.

The chameleons drift past
Fear who they really are.
Unable to make anything last.
Love and life
A stroke under par.

Perpetual seekers find nothing.
Optimists find everything.
Others live blissfully unfulfilled.
Pessimists see shadows in green hills.
Fatalists see everything willed.
Philosophers have a special wisdom.
Prophets find a higher kingdom.
But, who really knows?

Shades of grey can shift to crisp cold.
Not everything that glitters
Is worth to behold.
Old limbs holding generations,
Whisper in the receptive ear
Of forgotten, yet familiar, sensations.
Maybe for them the path is clear.

As we trip on our life's thread,
We might wonder
'Bout the things we have done and said.
Can it so easily be torn asunder?
It has to make you wonder.

Can answers be found in seas ever changing?
Resilience in willows ever bending.
Peace in rolling hills and valleys.
Reason in the shifting seasons.
Hope from the stars of the heavens.
Sorrow in grey days and highways.
Loneliness in the night.
Love and hate in sight.

Life can be shared with many people
But, find meaning with the people you love.

CHOICE

There is no, for better, or for worse,
Only what works.

No circumstances,
Only timing.

No regrets or lost opportunities,
Only what you choose to see.

If the shoe doesn't fit,
You crafted it.

Next time,
Reappraise the design.
Put together the pair
with the utmost care.

A fearful mind.
A resilient heart.
A rift, the sign
A partner accepts no part.

When to be together.
When to be apart.
When to know to finish.
When to know to start.

How to stop the expectations.
How to stop the many separations.
How to bring the scales to balance.
How to open a soul to the challenge.

To trust in life's tide.
To allow a buoyant spirit
To grow alongside.
To be fully alive.

RAGE

Fire through tinder-dry undergrowth.

Fast, Furious ... a behemoth.

Doused by cold revenge.

In the wake

Of retribution's break.

Fire through tinder-dry undergrowth.

Fast, Furious ...

FEAR AND HATRED

It,

Shows its ugliness,

Anger and frustration.

Nurtured in lonely places;

In dark unconscious spaces.

A person,

As a phantom, passes each day.

Some say they have lost their way.

It,

Seems to me,

Loneliness and despair.

A person afraid to care.

It,

Cannot hide

When there is no arrogant pride.

It,

Cannot flourish

In a world that cherishes.

It,

Cannot breed suspicion

Amongst people who share.

Live with a heart full of love;

A mind full of light.

Unveil the Id

Within full sight.

Watch **It,** transform.

Silence abandonment's rage.

In the sunny brilliance of self-acceptance.

No longer captive within *Its* cage.

TWILIGHT ZONE

At rest … alone.
To be with yourself
　And feel at home.

An Autumn breeze utters
My thoughts away.
Shielded, my eyes shuttered
　Into a twilight zone, I stray.

To a floating menagerie
In a cushion of white lace,
Illumined by candles of cold embrace,
　Shepherded by a lady's loving face.

Her mantle of white velvet spreads.
Cloaks the pain of what was done and said.
Invokes a call I cannot ignore.
　My spirit soothed, yet exposed and raw.

At rest,
No longer alone.
　Finally, I found home.

LIFE'S STAGE

Actors in a play,
We each mould our way.
Our performances, incomplete
Without another's contributing speech.

A sublime audience watches
Every move and inflection.
Many faces following lines to perfection.
The script, guidelines from the heart,
Act life out part by part.

The writer, and theatre's creation,
Construct worlds on a stage given sanction.
Imagination nurtured for those sensitive souls
committed to the artistry of their role.

NO FUTURE

Artificial buildings tastelessly ornamented.
One-armed machines lovingly ordained
  By clutching addicts
  In a tinder box atmosphere...

Eyes aflame,
Peer through grey mists
  Inhaled by the blackening lungs
  Of hangers on.

Now machines lie discarded.
People upgraded
  Their anecdotes of the past
  Enigmas for the future.

A sole palm tree stands sun-lit.
A forgotten flagpole in reverence
  To an old allegiance.
  Horizons only death did shift.

Now willows weep drops of gossamer
Over dead streams.
  Reflect images of a lost life,
  Forgotten dreams.

TURN THE PAGES

Bony fingers hold secrets within each turning
Carved by decades of fluctuant learning.
Guided by sight which cannot be taught,
But must be reached for and sort.

Light is solicited in dimensions all hallow,
Seeking protection from spectres and shadow.
Faith is loath to question the outer orbs.
Science ignores the inner corridors.

Souls are relinquished for the sake of religion.
Minds are bartered in the name of science.
Human nature provides the weapons
To destroy all works of wisdom and alliance.

Philosophy's ken lives in another sphere
Unburdened by acquiescence and fear.
For its knowledge you must reach high and search low,
To the height of your understanding
And the depth of your soul.
On many minds life will take its toll.

Strange doors will be looked for
In the lines of open pages.
Its key will not be found in established laws
But in the experiences of ages.

WORDS

Thoughts are forged;

The proud shaping of the finest sword.

Words flow too freely, short and sharp;

Daggers to pierce a vulnerable heart.

GOOD TIMES

Hardship infiltrates our very bones.
Good times skip and skim
But on the surface of our skin.

If not for the surface of the skin
Hardship would always infiltrate in.

A sunny layer
To battle joy's slayer,
And woe's soothsayer.

MISTY LINES

Words are being sung

Through the rhythms made.

Notes are gently flowing

Through a haze.

On winds wistfully blowing.

Through trees warmly glowing.

Elusive notes I must define,

Composed on misty lines.

❧